HELLO GOD

Do You Care?

Vickie Fisher

Author and Photographer

Copyright © 2022 by Vickie Fisher

Hello God, Do You Care?
by Vickie Fisher

Printed in the United States of America

ISBN: 978-1-7373842-2-9 (paperback)
ISBN: 978-1-7373842-3-6 (ebook)

All rights reserved solely by the author. The author guarantees all contents are original and do not infringe upon the legal rights of any other person or work. No part of this book may be reproduced in any form without the permission of the author.

Scriptures quotations marked (NIV) are taken from the Holy Bible, New International Version®, NIV®. Copyright © 1973, 1978, 1984, 2011 by Biblica, Inc.™ Used by permission of Zondervan. All rights reserved worldwide. www.zondervan.com The "NIV" and "New International Version" are trademarks registered in the United States Patent and Trademark Office by Biblica, Inc.™

Scripture quotations marked (TLB) are taken from The Living Bible copyright © 1971. Used by permission of Tyndale House Publishers, Carol Stream, Illinois 60188. All rights reserved.

Scripture quotations marked (ESV) are from The Holy Bible, English Standard Version® (ESV®), copyright © 2001 by Crossway, a publishing ministry of Good News Publishers. Used by permission. All rights reserved.

Scripture quotations marked (NKJV) are from the New King James Version®. Copyright © 1982 by Thomas Nelson, Inc. Used by permission. All rights reserved.

Scripture quotations marked (NLV) are from the New Life Version © Christian Literature International. Used by permission. All rights reserved.

ACKNOWLEDGMENTS

First and foremost, thank you God for allowing me to write this book, which I pray brings glory to Your name.

I would be remiss in not acknowledging the Bible and nature as both inspiring me to want to inspire you.

Without my editing team, this book would not be here, so I thank each of you from the bottom of my heart.

I am truly blessed to have such a loving family. They bring such joy to my life, a gift that proves God does care for me.

Most of the photographs in this book were taken on my nineteen acres. I am so grateful that God placed me in an environment where His beauty is so clearly visible. Photographs taken elsewhere include:

Page 12: Ocean City, MD

Page 24: Sherwood Gardens, Baltimore, MD

Page 30: Sherwood Gardens, Baltimore, MD

Page 50: Niagara Falls, Canada

Page 52: Howard County, MD

Page 56: Rhode Island—Cliff Walk

Page 58: Letchworth State Park, NY

Page 64: Skyline Drive, VA

Page 66: Howard County, MD

Page 74: Howard County, MD

Page 90: Ocean City, MD

Page 97: Howard County, MD

Page 100: Niagara Falls, Canada

DEDICATION

I dedicate this book to you.
My prayer is that each page will touch your soul
in such a way that you know God cares for you.

INTRODUCTION

Does God truly care about me? After all, in a world of over a trillion people, why would He care about one little person? Does He actually care about the little things going on in my life? There is only one answer to that question and it is yes. How do I know that?

My husband owned horses and before we got married he decided to make a new pasture behind the house. The fence posts were dug and it was time to put up the fencing. My husband Jerry put the first board on the outside of the post. His friend quickly jumped on that mistake because everyone knows the boards belong on the inside so the horses don't kick them off. Jerry said, "I want them to look pretty for Vickie." My heart filled with joy in that moment because I was loved.

Thirteen years later, Jerry died. I never realized how many times the horses kicked those boards off. Never once did he complain about the extra work the boards on the outside caused him. If he ever regretted placing them there, he never said. In my heart, I believe he never regretted it. But I did. Fixing those boards became just another burden of life without him.

Four years after Jerry died, I discovered the real reason those boards were placed on the outside of the post. I sold the horses and needed to mow the fields. I bought a new mower and wasn't sure how everything worked. I came off a hill and was going too fast and had no idea where the brake was so I crashed through the fence. The instant the boards broke outward, I knew that God told Jerry to put those boards on the outside. When I rolled off the mower and laid looking up at the sky, I thanked God and Jerry for saving my life. Because I knew that if the boards were on the other side, they would have broken inward, I would have been impaled, and my kids would be orphans. I now have a physical reminder where my broken wrist did not heal properly, that God does care about me. He looks ahead and knows what He needs to do to help keep me safe.

I am forever grateful that we have a God that cares about not just the big things, but even the little things.

Good morning, God. Thank you for this beautiful day. It doesn't matter what the weather looks like outside because I know that You blessed me with another day of life and You have good plans for me. Give me the strength and wisdom to embrace the challenges I might face, the grace to help others, and the directions to the path You laid ahead of me. I embrace today with joy and gratitude. I love today. Thank you.

Embrace Today

It is a gift

Have you ever hugged God? I have. No, I haven't hugged Him physically, but I do hug Him mentally. Before I open my eyes each morning, I visualize my arms around His wrist. I see His white robe and feel His arms wrapping themselves around me and my heart feels joy. When your day starts like this, how can it be bad? God's morning hug goes with me throughout the day, keeping my focus on what is good. You too can have this same moment with God. Reach out your arms and embrace Him.

*And so we know and rely on the love God has for us. God is love.
Whoever lives in love lives in God, and God in them.* I John 4:16 (NIV)

There are mornings when I wake up and high-five God for another day. Then there are the mornings where I stumble out of bed like a bear leaving hibernation. Those are the mornings I need to spread my arms in the air and twirl until the delight of a new day reaches my soul. Every day is a blessing no matter how it might seem. We are not alone. The Bible tells us that God has sent a helper to us, the Holy Spirit. He will help you through every struggle you face and rejoice with you in every triumph. Thank God for this day. Embrace it with the hopefulness of the rising sun.

Embrace Today

The steadfast love of the Lord never ceases; his mercies never come to an end;
they are new every morning; great is your faithfulness.
The Lord is my portion," says my soul, "therefore I will hope in him."
Lamentations 3:22-24 (ESV)

Each morning, as sleep releases you from its hold, embrace the day as the gift it is. Yesterday is gone, the door to tomorrow has not yet been opened, today is the day that matters. This moment, this hour has been gifted to you. How you react to it is your gift to yourself. No day is perfect. It's how we handle the issues that arise that determine if it will be a good day or not. We have all had those days where the second our feet hit the floor the day has already started spinning out of control. Stop, take a deep breath, and look for the beauty in the chaos. Today's challenges are molding you into the person God made you to be. Embrace the challenging days because they lead you to the perfect days.

Embrace Today

*Let the morning bring me word of your unfailing love,
for I have put my trust in you. Show me the way I should go,
for to you I entrust my life.* Psalm 143:8 (NIV)

Do you wonder if God cares about you, about this day? Why would He? You are just a speck in this huge world. The Bible says He does, that He knows every hair on your head. He takes care of the birds and the flowers so, of course, He's watching over you too. Today, as you start your day, remember you are blessed. God is standing by you, ready to shower your day with blessings. Claim this blessing for you and your family before you start each day.

May the Lord bless and protect you;
may the Lord's face radiate with joy because of you;
may he be gracious to you, show you his favor,
and give you his peace. Numbers 6:24-26 (TLB)

Dear Heavenly Father, do You cry when You look down upon us and see what an unaccepting world we have become? I know it hurts my heart. I can only imagine how You must feel. Please help us once again to learn to accept our differences. No one is always right or always wrong. Guide us to the middle ground where we can talk and sort out our differences without anger and condemnation. Please help me learn to leave the judging to You.

Acceptance

As you would like to be

Other than being human, you and I are not the same. We were never meant to be. Each one of us has our own unique and wonderful personality and talents to bring to the world. How boring would it be if every single person looked and thought alike? There would be nothing new because each one of us would have already thought of it. No surprises, no love. Nothing but the same thing day after day. This world we live in has become so jaded. If you don't agree with me, you can't be my friend. Instead of condemning each other's differences, we ought to be thankful for them. For in our differences is where new ideas and change grow.

Acceptance

Accept one another, then, just as Christ accepted you, in order to bring praise to God.
Romans 15:7 (NIV)

We live in a society where our past defines our present. Our cancel culture leaves no room for former mistakes. I wonder how many of us have said or done something twenty or more years ago that we would never think to say or do today. I know I have. In my past, I struggled with depression, which led me to say things I shouldn't have. I hated myself, which led me to abuse my body and mind. In my twenties, there were five years where I was mad at God and the world. I pray those years will never define who I am today.

Thankfully God is not like that. He has not only forgiven our sins, but has forgotten them. Where would we be if Ananias had refused to listen to God when He sent him to restore Saul of Tarsus's sight. Saul the murderer. If this was the present day, would we be so forgiving? Fortunately for us, he listened. He was not the judge, jury, and executioner. So Saul became the beloved Paul. God knows people can change. Next time you find yourself judging someone for their past, take a moment and ask yourself if this is who they are today. Are they forever stuck in the past like an unopened bud? Or have they taken their mistakes and turned their life into something meaningful? Accept them as they are today, letting go of their past failures, as you would like others to do for you.

Acceptance

Then all who heard were amazed, and said,
"Is this not he who destroyed those who called on this name in Jerusalem,
and has come here for that purpose, so that he might bring them bound to the chief priests?"
But Saul increased all the more in strength, and confounded the Jews who dwelt in Damascus,
proving that this Jesus is the Christ. Acts 9:21-22 (NKJV)

I cannot count the times I have asked God why He created me this way. Why aren't I as pretty as, why aren't I as smart as, why aren't I as talented as, and the list goes on. When I compare myself to others, I am not accepting the person God made me to be. He created every facet of me for His purpose, not mine. Accepting that truth means I have to rid myself of self-doubt and stop comparing myself to others. I need to thank God for creating me this way. Every single part of me, not just the ones I like. Accepting the fact that God made me "good enough" is my biggest struggle. If this is something you struggle with also, join me in saying this every morning, "I am good enough. I know this to be true because God said so." Who are we to doubt the Creator? He loved us enough to make us unique. Embrace who you are. Thank God for making you just the way you are.

Acceptance

*For You made the parts inside me. You put me together inside my mother.
I will give thanks to You, for the greatness of the way I was made brings fear.
Your works are great and my soul knows it very well.* Psalm 139:13-14 (NLV)

Dear Heavenly Father, I caught myself judging again. I know in my heart that woman did not deserve my judgment. I don't even know her. But watching the way she was acting, I found myself looking down on her as if I had never been in her shoes. I don't want to be that person who passes judgment on others. Please forgive me for my sin and fill my heart with love and not hate for those not like me. Thank You for caring about everyone and not just me.

Judgment
We are all created by God

Have you ever been drunk, taken illegal substances, had sex outside of marriage, over-eaten, under-eaten, lied, cheated, overspent, stolen, worn clothes too tight or too loose, lost your temper, been mean, made fun of someone, or made a bad decision? If you can say yes to just one of those, I have a question for you. Why are you judging someone else for something you have done? Judging others is an act of superiority. Are we better than others? None of us are perfect. I don't like being judged because it hurts. And when I find myself judging others, my heart feels sick. Often we find ourselves judging people we don't even know. Like maybe that person in church who reeks of alcohol? Instead of judging them, be glad they are there. Unlike many others, they felt the desire to hear God's word. Instead of judgment, give them a smile and a word of kindness. It might be all they need to reach for Jesus. Even if you are only judging them in your head, God hears your thoughts. When I find myself starting to judge someone, I quickly pray for them and for myself—them for God's help and myself for forgiveness.

Judgment

"Do not judge, or you too will be judged. For in the same way you judge others, you will be judged, and with the measure you use, it will be measured to you. "Why do you look at the speck of sawdust in your brother's eye and pay no attention to the plank in your own eye? Matthew 7:1-3 (NIV)

God lovingly created each one of us. He did not ask if I wanted to be born in America or a third-world country. He didn't ask if I wanted to be born white or another color. He did not ask if I wanted to be rich or poor. Why? Because my answers didn't change who He made me to be. The entire earth is God's garden and the people in it are His flowers. Think about that for a moment. Each one of us is God's flower meant to bloom where He planted us. Not by our choice, but His. This world is full of hatred of anyone different than us. Ask yourself, "Why do I hate these people? Is it because I know firsthand that every single person from that group is bad, or is it because I have listened to what others are saying about them?" When we judge others, we are saying we are superior. Nowhere in the Bible does it say God created anyone superior to another. It does say we are to love others, not just those like us. When we hate someone because of where they were born, we are saying God made a mistake. God does not make mistakes. Hatred puts a wall between you and God. Break through that wall, open your heart, and have compassion for those less fortunate than you. The most beautiful gardens are those filled with a variety of flowers. Love for others is the most beautiful flower in God's garden and He has given it to all of us.

Judgment

"The most important one," answered Jesus, "is this: 'Hear, O Israel:
The Lord our God, the Lord is one. Love the Lord your God with all your heart
and with all your soul and with all your mind and with all your strength.
The second is this: 'Love your neighbor as yourself.'
There is no commandment greater than these." Mark 12:29-31 (NIV)

Dear Heavenly Father, here I am again, stressed out to the point I can't think straight. The more I try not to worry, the more I worry. It's a never-ending fight I can't seem to win. Please clear my mind and put my focus back on You and not my problems. Help me remember You are walking beside me every moment of every day. Thank You for releasing me from the burden of worry and restoring peace to me.

Worry

Give it to God

I have been asked many times, "Don't you care about anything?" Of course, I do. Do I worry – no. I hate worrying because it gets me so tied up in knots I can't think straight. So I don't worry. How is that possible? When I was younger, I used to joke that if I had a problem, I would tell my mother and she would worry about it. There was no sense in the two of us worrying over it. Was that selfish of me? Sort of, but whether I worried or not, she was going to, no matter what. After she died, when worry came, I would ask myself, "Is this something I have control over?" If not, I handed it over to Jesus. I completely trust Him to handle the situation. I have never been able to change anything by worrying about it. To me, worry is a waste of energy. There is so much more to do in life than spend even a minute worrying over something that might happen. Put it on a shelf and leave it there until the time arrives that you have to face it. Better yet, hand it over to Jesus, the Master of all things. He has this. Enjoy the beauty of a worry-free life.

Worry

Who of you by worrying can add a single hour to your life?
Since you cannot do this very little thing, why do you worry about the rest?
Luke 12:25-26 (NIV)

Stress is an elevated version of worry. It is not your friend. It is an ugly demon coming to wreak havoc on your life and slowly destroy your body. Like all enemies, this one can be destroyed. How? First, by praying and focusing on this moment, not the what ifs. If you are in the middle of a crisis, don't allow stress to cloud your judgment and run away with your emotions. You might be thinking: *Easy for you to say, you don't stress.* You're right, I don't. I learned stress management from my dad. I can't tell you how many times I heard, "Let's see what tomorrow brings." He lived in the moment, never stressing about what was coming or worrying about what happened yesterday. Today, this moment, was what mattered. The rest would show up when it was supposed to and he would handle it if and when it did. For me, when I feel stress rising inside, I pray and ask for guidance. Then I look out the window and calm myself with nature and stress disappears. We have enough troubles in our lives without adding stress to the mix. Jesus has promised to help us in all things. Allow Him to take your stress away. He cares about you.

Worry

Lord, when doubts fill my mind, when my heart is in turmoil, quiet me and give me renewed hope and cheer. Psalm 94:19 (TLB)

Like a sly demon sneaking into our minds, anxiety can quickly take hold and knock us to our knees. If we aren't careful, it can break us to the point of death. Stress is a silent killer wreaking havoc inside of our bodies. What if, what if, what if—keeps you in a constant state of worry. When we allow stress to invade our minds, we are saying to God, "I am in control, not You." It is only when we hand everything over to Him that we can breathe freely. There is nothing too big for God to handle. He cares about you. He wants you to have a joyful life. Reach to the sky and declare yourself free of worry. God has this.

Worry

O God, you have declared me perfect in your eyes;
you have always cared for me in my distress;
now hear me as I call again.
Have mercy on me. Hear my prayer.
Psalm 4:1 (TLB)

    Hello God, if you care, why do I have to face yet another trial? I'm so weary of the struggles. I just want them to be over. I know You have not promised a life of ease, but some of us have more than our fair share of issues. Just for today, I ask You to rid me of this burden and to give me the strength and knowledge to be able to face what life is throwing at me. Help me realize that the troubles I am facing are nothing that You can't handle. Take my hand and walk with me through this day.

Life's Trials
You can do this

If you look closely, you will see that nature has a way of mirroring our lives. The ebb and flow of this tiny stream changes with the seasons. In the summer, it bubbles over, making a sweet sound of joy. Other times, there is barely a trickle of life left in it. Along comes winter and the water freezes. The ebb and flow of life are just like that. Sometimes we are bubbling over with joy, then the harsh winds of adversity threaten to freeze us in place. But unlike the stream, we do not have to be frozen. When we face hardship as a challenge and not an enemy, we become stronger. God has placed within each of us the strength to defeat the enemy. No matter what life throws at you today, you have this. God has faith in you.

Life's Trials

*God is our refuge and strength, a tested help in times of trouble.
And so we need not fear even if the world blows up
and the mountains crumble into the sea.* Psalm 46:1-2 (TLB)

When I took this photograph, I couldn't help but wonder: *Why are those leaves still hanging on? Do they not know the cycle of their lives?* Beauty in the spring as they bud into being, shade in the hot days of summer, then once again a burst of splendor right before they fall to the ground. Yet, these leaves decided to hang on. For what purpose, I do not know. Maybe it was just so I could get this beautiful picture. Or maybe they are like us, clinging to the past as if we can change the outcome. How is new life supposed to emerge if, like the leaf, we become frozen in the past? Release the hold of the past and embrace the warmth of today.

"Forget the former things; do not dwell on the past. See, I am doing a new thing! Now it springs up; do you not perceive it? I am making a way in the wilderness and streams in the wasteland." Isaiah 43:18-19 (NIV)

Every day is full of those "oops" moments. Gossiping, overeating, addictions, laziness, and anger are all sins we often brush to the side with a "shouldn't have done that. Oh well, I am only human." And like a fox, sin has crept in and devoured your peace. Those so-called little sins have as much power to put a cloud between you and God as the bigger sins do, maybe even more so. When we commit what we recognize as a major sin, we quickly go to God for forgiveness. When these little everyday sins happen, we don't even think about it. We discount them as human nature and with that comes the problem. If you feel as if there is a barrier between you and God, ask Him to show you what sins you have been committing without realizing it. No matter how small or big it is, God will help you change and remove that cloud blocking out your peace.

Life's Trials

*"For all have sinned and fall short of the glory of God,
and are justified by his grace as a gift,
through the redemption that is in Christ Jesus."*
Romans 3:23-24 (ESV)

Dear Heavenly Father, I am screaming out to You for help. I thought I was doing well, but then I got frustrated, which made me angry, and now I'm disappointed in myself and the tornado of my emotions threatens to defeat me. I don't want to feel so out of control. Please take this emotional mayhem from me and restore to me the peace I can only find in You.

Emotional Mayhem
Release control

Emotional mayhem comes in different forms. It may show itself with impatience, frustration, disappointment, or anger. What they all have in common is the lack of control we feel due to something or someone around us. Life is full of out-of-our-control moments. Maybe you didn't get the job or win first place, maybe your child is throwing a temper tantrum, maybe who you thought loved you didn't, and the list goes on. Everything, including traffic, has to do with someone else. Changing the outcome may never happen, but changing your attitude can. When you feel mayhem spring up inside of you, stomp it to the ground. Close your eyes and whisper a quick prayer asking for help. Nothing in your past has defeated you; neither will this.

Emotional Mayhem

Anxiety weighs down the heart, but a kind word cheers it up.
Proverbs 12:25 (NIV)

Have you ever gotten so angry to the point you threw something? You are not alone. Take a look at Moses. He spent forty days and nights in the presence of God. He saw Him, talked to Him, and watched the hand of God write the Ten Commandants on a tablet of stone. Then when Moses came down from the mountain and saw what the Israelites were doing, he got so mad that he threw the tablet with enough force to break it. Can you imagine how Moses must have felt having to go back up the mountain and face God? As hard as that must have been, Moses did what he was told and was forgiven. How do we know for sure he was forgiven? Multiple times in the New Testament, Moses is seen with Elijah and Jesus. God knows our faults and He loves us anyway. Will we be forgiven? Yes. Will we have to face discipline for our wrongs? Yes. Moses was human just like us. He was created for a purpose just like we are. When we slip, we ask for forgiveness and it is done. It really is that easy. Ask God to take that rage from you. Ask Him to help you control your temper the next time you feel it brewing inside of you. God cares about you. He wants you to live a life flowing with peace. He will give it to you. Just ask Him.

Emotional Mayhem

Stop being mean, bad-tempered, and angry.
Quarreling, harsh words, and dislike of others should have no place in your lives.
Instead, be kind to each other, tenderhearted, forgiving one another,
just as God has forgiven you because you belong to Christ.
Ephesians 4:31-32 (TLB)

Guilt is one of those pesky demons that shows up unannounced. Somewhere in your past, you have done something you aren't proud of. It could be something major or something most people would just brush off, but your actions were so out of character for you that years later it still haunts you. You have asked God for forgiveness, and yet guilt arrives without warning, filling your heart with remorse. Was this sin so bad that God can't forgive it? That is actually what Satan wants you to think. He used guilt as a barrier between you and peace. We all have done things we aren't proud of. There is nothing we can do to change that. But know God has forgiven you. When guilt arrives, call out to Jesus and ask Him to take your mind off of this sin and shift it back on Him. You are not the same person you were. We all change and do not need to carry the burden of the past with us. Release it into the hands of Jesus. He already paid the price.

Emotional Mayhem

*Come, let's talk this over, says the Lord;
no matter how deep the stain of your sins,
I can take it out and make you as clean as freshly fallen snow.
Even if you are stained as red as crimson,
I can make you white as wool!*
Isaiah 1:18 (TLB)

Patience is one of those things you think you have plenty of until it's gone. One unforeseen problem, one nasty remark, one more delay, and *poof,* it's gone. We are not alone. The Bible is full of grumbling and impatience. We might not have to wait forty years to get where we are going, but we do still need to wait on God's timing. Next time you are stuck in traffic, thank God for the delay. You don't know what He is saving you from. Next time your child throws a fit, instead of losing your patience along with theirs, hug them. What looks to you like nothing could very well be major to them. Patience is not a two-way street. Patience is about you, and others will need to deal with their own issues. Impatience destroys not only your mood, but the moods of those around you. When you feel the tide of impatience flowing over you, take a deep breath. Do not allow it to pull you under. Grab hold of patience like a gem from God.

Emotional Mayhem

Be completely humble and gentle; be patient, bearing with one another in love.
Ephesians 4:2 (NIV)

Frustration is one of life's little demons that likes to rear its ugly head over and over again. If we saw it coming, it would be so much easier to squash, but it slowly builds until it explodes inside of us. This is the tool Satan uses most often on me and let me assure you it's not pretty when it shows up. I am ranting and raving, crying, and all but giving up. I can just see Satan now, tapping God on the shoulder, laughing, and asking, "What do you think of her now?" God just smiles because He knows that He has given me the fortitude to try again. And try again I do. Frustration isn't the real issue. The problem comes with our feeling of being inadequate, which leads us to feel hopeless. Life will throw many things at us that we are not equipped to handle. Yet. We don't have to be like the fountain that allowed the ice to build up around it until it was a mountain. Look closely at the top of the fountain and you will see the water still emerging. It triumphed over what seemed impossible. You can too. When you feel frustration wrapping itself around you, take a step back, take a deep breath, and remember inside of you is the ability to conquer this too.

So I find this law at work: Although I want to do good, evil is right there with me. For in my inner being I delight in God's law; but I see another law at work in me, waging war against the law of my mind and making me a prisoner of the law of sin at work within me. What a wretched man I am! Who will rescue me from this body that is subject to death? Thanks be to God, who delivers me through Jesus Christ our Lord! So then, I myself in my mind am a slave to God's law, but in my sinful nature a slave to the law of sin. Romans 7:21-25 (NIV)

Emotional Mayhem

The biggest lie we are ever told is that words will not hurt us. Yes, "sticks and stones may break our bones," but words have the power to destroy a person as surely as a bullet through the heart. How many adults are still broken by words spoken to them in childhood? How many dreams have been shattered by words like a knife slashing through paper? Words can kill, destroying a person bit by bit until nothing is left but the shell of the person they were meant to be. I strive to be a kind person who always looks for the good in someone, but I too have said words that had the power to harm another person, and that breaks my heart. I pray that each of us is given an extra dose of kindness and understanding today. With God's help and loving words, together we can make this world a better place.

Emotional Mayhem

Your own soul is nourished when you are kind; it is destroyed when you are cruel.
Proverbs 11:17 (TLB)

Dear Heavenly Father, I am lost and so afraid. The darkness is closing in on me and I fear there is no way out. I want to lean on You, but today I feel so hopeless that I'm not even sure if You are there. My heart is overflowing with pain, my shoulders have too much to carry, and my thoughts are swirling waves of darkness. I don't know if I can go on. Please hear my cry of despair. Today, more than ever, I need You. I am begging for You to reach into the darkness with even just a ray of hope. Show me the way back into the light.

Despair
You are loved

If you are reading this and your heart is so full of despair that you see no way out but death, please hear my plea. You are loved. Someone cares about you. You will be missed. Death is not the answer. Inside of you is the strength to get up and fight. You may not feel it at this moment, but I promise you it is there. Jesus has embraced you and wants you to live. I want you to live. Please know that your life matters. At this moment, you may not feel like it does, but it does. There is nothing that can't be fixed. Nothing that you can't move past. Yes, it will be hard, but you can do this. Here is the number for the national suicide hotline, **800-273-8255**. Please call for help. If not for yourself, do me a favor and call for me. I may not know you personally, but I pray for you every day. My prayer is that God will send His angels to lift you out of the pit of darkness and back into His loving light.

Despair

I waited patiently for God to help me; then he listened and heard my cry.
He lifted me out of the pit of despair, out from the bog and the mire,
and set my feet on a hard, firm path, and steadied me as I walked along.
He has given me a new song to sing, of praises to our God.
Now many will hear of the glorious things he did for me,
and stand in awe before the Lord, and put their trust in him.
Psalm 40:1-3 (TLB)

I was fourteen the first time I heard someone say they wanted to die. Fortunately, I took her seriously and was able to convince my father that she had taken some pills and we needed to find her. I will never forget the headlights of his car shining on her white sweater laying in the weeds. My heart still gasps at the memory all these years later. That first attempt, and many others through the years, left scars not just on her, but on the family that loved her. It took years, but she finally was able to get help and live a good life. And yes, Christians can and do get depressed. Did you know that Moses asked God to take his life and Elijah ran from his problems and wanted to die? Other great men in the Bible faced depression so deep they wanted to die too. But God had other plans. Whether you are the one thinking of taking your own life or the loved one feeling helpless to help, know that God is with you even in this time of darkness. He loves you, and just like He did for Elijah and Moses, He is there to help you. Call out to Him in your despair and give your heartaches and disappointments to Him. He is waiting to lift you from the pit of darkness and back into the light of day.

Despair

*May the God of hope fill you with all joy and peace as you trust in him,
so that you may overflow with hope by the power of the Holy Spirit.*
Romans 15:13 (NIV)

This world is too full of men and women from all walks of life, fighting what they believe to be the losing battle of addiction. It isn't a losing battle. Ask the millions of people who have proven they could quit. It doesn't matter if it's drugs, alcohol, or something else—you can break free. Will it be easy when the pull of addiction comes knocking on your door, taunting you to do it just one more time? No, but you have within yourself the power to walk away. There are two doors in front of you. One leads to darkness, self-hatred, and despair. The other leads to freedom, love, and salvation. If you are reading these words, then you haven't lost all hope. Please reach out for help, **1-800-662-HELP (4357)**, then turn to Jesus. He might not be walking the earth in His physical body, but He is still here. And just like He healed thousands of people in His day, He is still doing it today. If you think your addiction has made you unworthy for Him to heal you, think again. Never once did Jesus ask those He healed if they were worthy. He willingly healed them of all kinds of diseases. Addictions are cancers eating away at you. Reach out your hand and ask to be released from this disease and to have the courage to defeat this plague destroying you. Please don't continue down this road of despair. Take your life back. You are strong enough. You are loved.

Despair

*No temptation has overtaken you except what is common to mankind.
And God is faithful; he will not let you be tempted beyond what you can bear.
But when you are tempted, he will also provide a way out so that you can endure it.*
I Corinthians 10:13 (NIV)

A dear friend of my family was addicted to heroin. I asked him what made him pick up that needle the very first time, knowing what it was about to do to him. What he said broke my heart. He said he didn't care if he lived or died. He just wanted to feel good. Addiction is a slow form of suicide. You might not die today or tomorrow, but your addiction is slowly killing you and your family. Every time you feed your addiction, a fog of uncertainty covers you and your family. Will this be the end? If you have been lied to like my friend and told that you can't kick the habit, I assure you, you can. If one other person has done it, why can't you? Is it because you feel unworthy, lost, or all alone? You aren't. Jesus was tempted by Satan. What did He do? He said, "Away from me, Satan!" You can use those same words. Your addiction is the work of the devil. You wouldn't willingly invite him into your life, but that is what you are doing every time you feed your addiction, which is why it is so hard to quit. Once Satan has a stronghold on you, he is not willing to let go. That is why you need Jesus. He has crushed Satan. He has conquered everything evil in this world. He can and will defeat your addiction. Next time you feel the pull of Satan, call on Jesus and allow Him to defeat the enemy and restore your life to the glorious one He has planned for you.

Despair

And their prayer, if offered in faith, will heal him, for the Lord will make him well;
and if his sickness was caused by some sin, the Lord will forgive him.
Admit your faults to one another and pray for each other so that you may be healed.
The earnest prayer of a righteous man has great power and wonderful results.
James 5:15-16 (TLB)

Dear Heavenly Father, I cry out to You in anguish. My heart is heavy, my steps are slow, and it takes every ounce of strength to get out of bed. I can't take this loss. You promised to comfort me, but I don't feel it. All I feel is suffocating grief. I lift myself and those walking through this valley of death into Your hands. Bring Your angels to comfort us as we navigate through this dark void of hopelessness. Allow us to feel Your presence so we know we are not alone.

Grief
Love never dies

I can remember the darkest moment of my life as if it was yesterday and not twenty-two years ago. The news that my husband had a massive heart attack and was dead swept over me like a tidal wave of darkness knocking me to my knees. I screamed, "NO," and sank to the floor in uncontrollable sobs. How could this be? He was the healthiest person I knew. This was not real. I could hear voices trying to soothe me, but it wasn't their voices that cut through the despair. Something inside of me whispered, *"All is not lost."* So, I stood up and faced the ordeal ahead of me. The next few hours were a blur. The one thing that stands out for me is something the chaplain said, "You are going to be okay. I have watched you and I can see that you have an inner strength that will get you through this." I remember thinking: *I have you fooled*. But it was me who was fooled. I thought that because I cried and felt empty, I was weak. Emotions are not a sign of weakness. They are a sign of living. In my darkest hour, when grief threatened to destroy me, it was Jesus who picked me up off that floor and gave me the strength to go on. Do not think because you are knocked to the ground that you will not overcome this. You will, one moment at a time. You have the greatest Comforter there with you.

He heals the brokenhearted and binds up their wounds.
Psalm 147:3 (NIV)

The hardest thing I have ever had to bear was grief, and not just from death. Grief is just as real from the loss of a relationship as it is from death. The intense feeling of helplessness wraps its ugly arms around us and threatens to suffocate the life right out of us. Those around us don't offer the comfort or understanding as they would after a death. But many of us have at some point in time felt this near debilitating plunge into darkness. When my first marriage ended, it took me five years to climb out of the pit of darkness it had thrown me into. My faith in God was shattered. My faith in love was gone. My shame at my failure was invisibly stamped on my forehead like a scarlet letter. My saving grace was my son. Without him, I would not have cared about anything. It was prayer that lifted me out of the pits of hell. Next time you see someone struggling with grief, say a prayer on their behalf to lift them from their darkness.

The Lord is close to the brokenhearted and saves those who are crushed in spirit.
Psalm 34:18 (NIV)

Grief

I wish I could tell you that grief goes away, but it doesn't. Will the swirling waves of darkness dim in time? Yes, but go away completely, no. Each time a loved one dies, a part of us dies too. We know our parents will most likely die before us, but when they do, it is always too soon. It has been years since my mother died, and yet I still find myself wanting to call her. Since nothing is impossible for God, I send a prayer to Heaven and ask Him to send one of His angels to hug her for me. I truly believe He does that because my heart suddenly feels light and a bit more of my grief is released and replaced by the knowledge that she is only gone from my reach, not God's.

Grief

*We are confident, yes, well pleased rather to be absent from the body
and to be present with the Lord.*
II Corinthians 5:8 (NKJV)

Hello God, here I am again crying out for forgiveness. How many times have I confessed the same sins over and over? I know You forgave me the first time I asked, so I know the problem is not with You, but with me. I can't forgive myself. The sins of my life seem to be on a continuous loop like a bad movie you don't want to watch, but can't seem to turn off. Every lie I have ever told going back into my childhood, the time I helped someone cheat to pass a test, the gossip I spread, my behavior in "my wild years." The list goes on and on. Please teach me how to forgive myself and clean the cloudy screen blocking me from the joy of Your forgiveness.

Forgiveness
Will set you free

Forgiving someone is hard. The pain they have inflicted on you is real, whether it be emotionally, physically, or mentally. However, the real suffering comes when you don't forgive them. Maybe not right away, maybe not for years, but unforgiveness festers inside of you, damaging you more than the initial attack. Your heart and mind become frozen in time, blocked from trusting, loving, or being free. Jesus tells us to forgive one another. He never said it would be easy. Life is not easy, but it is the only way you will be free to move on.

Forgiveness

For if you forgive other people when they sin against you, your heavenly Father will also forgive you. Matthew 6:14 (NIV)

One of the hardest things to do is to forgive yourself. How many times have you, like me, found yourself praying for forgiveness for the same thing? I know that the first time I asked God, He wiped the slate clean. And yet, I find myself praying again and again. I can almost see God shaking His head. That sin is gone. But it's not gone for me and that is where the problem lies. When I won't forgive myself, I put a barrier of doubt between me and God. When you find yourself asking for forgiveness for something you know that God already forgave you for, pray instead for the power to forgive yourself. God loves you and wants you to be free from all guilt and shame.

Forgiveness

*Now, when sins have once been forever forgiven and forgotten,
there is no need to offer more sacrifices to get rid of them.
And so, dear brothers, now we may walk right into the very Holy of Holies,
where God is, because of the blood of Jesus.* Hebrews 10:18-19 (TLB)

There have been moments in my life where I needed to forgive God. What? God has done nothing wrong. How can you forgive God? You're right, He hasn't done anything wrong, but there are plenty of things in my life that He could have changed, but didn't. How many trials does one person have to go through? Did I need another heartache? Another injury? Loss of pay? Why am I never good enough? When do I get to break through to success? We each have our own list of struggles, whether they are finances, mental, physical, or emotional. When we look at them from our point of view, we can easily get lost in being mad at God. After all, He could have given us a perfect life. Every heartache or challenge could have easily been taken care of, but He didn't. Do I forgive God? NO! The forgiveness is not of God, it is of me for not trusting that every uphill battle is placed not to defeat me, but to grow me into the person God trusts me to become. As I walk through the fire of life, I look not into myself, but upward to the Heavens and lean on God to guide my path. Forgive me for my lack of faith in my times of trouble.

Forgiveness

*Although the Lord gives you the bread of adversity and the water of affliction,
your teachers will be hidden no more; with your own eyes you will see them.
Whether you turn to the right or to the left, your ears will hear a voice behind you, saying,
"This is the way; walk in it." Isaiah 30:20-21 (NIV)*

Dear Heavenly Father, I lift up to You the people of the world. As I look around, I see a plague of distrust more powerful than the COVID-19 pandemic. Everywhere there is sickness, loneliness, distrust, and death, not only of life, but of hope. I pray for the reader of these words that they will not allow the turmoil of the world to destroy their hope. Restore in them the knowledge that nothing is too hard for You to overcome. Thank You, Jesus, for giving us hope, for loving us, and for caring for each one of us.

Hope
There is always hope

Hope is like the rays of the sun showing us the way out of the darkness. Struggles will come, but just as we have in the past, we can overcome them. As of today, you have faced and defeated every challenge thrown in your way. Many were not easy, but you did it. Why would today be any different? Do not get lost in the struggles, instead welcome the lessons you are learning. Cling to hope, and like the rising sun, you too will shine bright.

"For I know the plans I have for you," declares the Lord,
"plans to prosper you and not to harm you, plans to give you hope and a future."
Jeremiah 29:11 (NIV)

I can not tell you how many times I have shouted, "I am not Job. I can't take this anymore." And yet, I have overcome every struggle, every heartache, and every injury. It has not been easy and there have been moments when I just wanted to rant and rave and give up. And to be honest, I have. But deep inside of me there has always been this tiny ray of hope that pulls me up out of the darkness. Troubles happen to each one of us. We think we have everything under control, then like a blast of winter air, we are frozen in place. Hope is what warms our hearts and carries us through the storm. There is always hope. Cling to it, as your life depends on it.

Hope

Be joyful in hope, patient in affliction, faithful in prayer.
Romans 12:12 (NIV)

A dream is hope's way of reminding us that it's not too late. You are never too old or too young to reach for your dreams. I can still remember getting my first camera at eight years old. Were the pictures memorable? No, but the joy of receiving that first camera and snapping my first picture was. I truly believe at that moment God planted within me the desire to create these books. Around the same time, I wanted to be a missionary. That never happened… or so I thought. I have come to realize these books are my mission. Is it the way I had dreamt all those years ago? No, but God had another plan, a plan that used all my dreams in a way so much better than what I had hoped for. What are your dreams? I know in my heart that what God has instilled inside of you, you can achieve. Reach for your dreams. Let hope find its way home to you.

Hope

*The Lord will work out his plans for my life
—for your loving-kindness, Lord, continues forever.
Don't abandon me—for you made me.*
Psalm 138:8 (TLB)

Dear Heavenly Father, thank You for this life You have given me... with all its bumps and bruises and all the wonderful blessings You have bestowed on me. Thank You for showing me over and over again how much You care for me.

Caring

God cares for you

Have you ever prayed, begged, and pleaded with God for something, only to have the answer be no? Then months or even years later, you discover what you thought you wanted really wasn't what you wanted. That was God caring for you. We see the short term, but He sees everything. Next time you receive that no, thank God for it. Even if you don't feel it now, you will. Thank Him for caring enough about you to not give you everything you beg for.

Caring

"For My thoughts are not your thoughts, Nor are your ways My ways," says the Lord. "For as the heavens are higher than the earth, So are My ways higher than your ways, and My thoughts than your thoughts. Isaiah 55:8-9 (NKJV)

How many times have we heard: "Trust your gut?" I have come to realize that gut instinct isn't coming from me, it is the Holy Spirit guiding me to the right decisions. What looks like the right thing to do to us doesn't always mean it is. We see only what is in front of us, but God sees the whole picture. Years ago, I was excited to buy a business. I had assured the owners that if I was able to get the financing, I would buy them out. When the banker told me I was approved, I felt a pit forming in my stomach. I should have been happy, but I wasn't. The banker shocked me by advising me not to go ahead with it. But this was my golden opportunity. This business was booming. How could I go wrong? He actually asked me to think about it before signing any papers. So I did and every time I thought about it, I literally got sick. I ended up turning it down. Within five years, that business failed. If I hadn't trusted my gut, I would have lost everything, starting with my home. Would a God that didn't care about you have sent the Holy Spirit to direct your path? Next time your intuition tells you something, look above and thank God for caring about you.

Caring

"Give all your worries and cares to God, for he cares about you."
I Peter 4:7 (NLT)

Can prayer change the world? I believe it can. Moses convinced God not to destroy the Israelites, just by asking Him not to. Yes, Moses had direct access to God, but so do we through Jesus. I truly believe that if all believers pray for the evil in this world to end, it will. Together we have the power to stop Satan in his tracks. There is so much goodness in this world that is being swallowed up with evil. Let us join together and bring kindness, compassion, and love back to the forefront. Let's pray for discernment and faith. Let the healing of the world begin today with each one of us. Together we can bring beauty back into the world. I know this because God cares for each one of us. It doesn't matter where you are at this moment. You should believe that God cares not only about the world, but also for you. He hears your voice, knows your problems, and is here to mend them. Miracles are out there just waiting for your prayers to grab hold of them. God can chase the darkness from this world and bring beauty back to it. We just need to ask.

Caring

*"Again, truly I tell you that if two of you on earth agree about anything they ask for,
it will be done for them by my Father in heaven.
For where two or three gather in my name, there am I with them."*
Matthew 18:19-20 (NIV)

There is nothing the enemy wants more than to see you defeated and ashamed. How often does he forget that Jesus overcame the world? There is nothing other than not accepting Jesus as your Savior that will keep you from the love of God. God loves you so much that He sent His only begotten Son to die for you. If you were the only person on this earth, Jesus would have still gotten up on that cross for you. Wow, just think about that for a moment. Let those words wrap themselves around your heart and soul. Feel the power the death of Jesus bought to you. Yes, you. The enemy can tempt you, he can lead you astray, but he can never defeat you again. God promised that once you belong to Him, nothing can take you away. Open your heart to the greatest love there ever is, Jesus.

Caring

For God so loved the world that he gave his one and only Son,
that whoever believes in him shall not perish but have eternal life.
John 3:16 (NIV)

Thank you for reading *Hello God, Do You Care?* I may not know your name, but rest assured I will be praying for you tonight as I do for all my readers. I pray you find the strength to handle whatever problems you are facing and that you too will see the love of God pouring out from above in the beauty of His nature, proving how much He cares for you.

Other Books by Vickie Fisher

Hello God, Are You There?
Hello God, It's Me Again
Hello God, Can You Hear Me?

Contact me at Vickie.fisher@verizon.net
Web page: Vickiefisher.com

www.ingramcontent.com/pod-product-compliance
Lightning Source LLC
Chambersburg PA
CBHW050739110526
44590CB00002B/23